Helping Young Children to Think Creatively

ACKNOWLEDGEMENTS

Written by: Ros Bayley & Lynn Broadbent

Illustrated by: Peter Scott

Produced & Published by: Lawrence Educational
                            Unit 21, Brookvale Trading Estate,
                            Birmingham B6 7AQ

                            © Lawrence Educational 2002

ISBN: 978-1-903670-14-9

INTRODUCTION

All of us have the ability to think creatively, but the extent to which we do will probably be highly dependent on the quality of our earliest experiences. If, in early childhood, we have been fortunate enough to have spent time in the company of creative adults, then generating new and original ideas will probably have become a way of life. Children learn by listening, watching and copying, and when they see the adults around them 'thinking outside of the box', they will invariably grow to respond to situations in a similar way. Whilst some aspects of creativity may be genetically endowed, there is little doubt in our minds that creativity can also be cultivated.

With the right stimulus and support all children can learn to think in ways that enable them to solve problems, be inventive and make discoveries, but this does not happen by osmosis. It requires thought, planning and imagination. Children need to be presented with situations that fire their curiosity and promote wonder and puzzlement, and that is the purpose of this book.

The ideas vary from 'easy to implement' to 'mildly more adventurous and challenging', and in keeping with creative thought, there is no single right way to use this book. Leaf through the pages and pick out the ideas that capture your imagination. Don't be afraid to take a few risks as this is central to creative thinking. If things don't work out the way you want them to, go back to the drawing board and have another bash, for in truth, some of our greatest learning happens when we make mistakes!

Whatever happens, enjoy yourself and remember, the amount we learn is commensurate with the amount of fun we are having. Have a great time problem solving, speculating and generating creative ideas!

Ros Bayley & Lynn Broadbent

ACTIVITY 1.

The teddy in the tree

RESOURCES:

A teddy bear, a label and for the really adventurous, a small parachute.

PROCESS:

Write a message on the label and tie it to the teddy bear. It may say something like 'Please help this bear. He is lost and has nowhere to live.' Then conceal the bear in a bush or a tree for the children to discover. Once they have found him, hold a special meeting to think about how you will respond to the situation. Encourage the children to think about where he has come from, why he is lost and what they might do to help him. Start an interactive display to chart the process of the project. Photograph him in the tree (and in various other places!) Caption the photographs with the children's thoughts and feelings. Write a letter to the children from someone who has lost a bear. Could it be the same bear or purely coincidence? Listen carefully to the children's responses, let your imagination flow and see where the project takes you.

ACTIVITY 2. # The Golden Eggs

RESOURCES:

Some straw and leaves to make a nest, some hard-boiled eggs and some gold spray or paint.

PROCESS:

Paint or spray the eggs gold and make a nest from the straw and the leaves. Once you have done this find a good place in the outside area or garden to conceal your nest, and wait for the children to discover it. Once found, they can speculate about how it got there, draw pictures of the creature they think laid the eggs and talk about whether they think the eggs will hatch. Encourage them to feel the eggs and decide upon a good place to keep them. Monitor their progress. Listen carefully to the children's comments and respond appropriately!

ACTIVITY 3.   # The Mysterious Footprints

RESOURCES:

Some brown water based paint and a footprint template.

PROCESS:

When the children have gone home and it looks as if it's not going to rain overnight, paint footprints on the ground in the outside area. Start them by a bush and take them to a door, or to another clump of bushes, or let them disappear around a corner. Listen carefully to what the children have to say when they discover them. Add your own suggestions as to how they got there and to whom they belong. Repeat the exercise after an interval of time and encourage the children to speculate, predict and imagine.

ACTIVITY 4.

The Dog's Collar

RESOURCES:

A dog's collar with a name tag on.

PROCESS:

Explain to the children that you found the collar on the pavement / fence etc. on your way to school. Encourage them to speculate about what the animal might have been like (this will be dictated by the size and type of the collar and influenced by the name on the tag.) Get the children to think about who might have owned the animal and why it is no longer wearing its collar. Discuss ideas about what should happen to the collar. Talk about the owner and how he or she might be feeling.

ACTIVITY 5.

The Presents

RESOURCES:

A large box, some balloons, a medium size box, something that rattles, a small box and something heavy, some wrapping paper.

PROCESS:

Wrap up the presents ensuring that in some cases you create the effect of something that doesn't fit! Tell the children that someone has left them (or you!) some presents and that you have no idea what is inside them. Encourage the children to offer their ideas about what is inside the boxes and who they think wrapped them up. As they offer their ideas encourage them to explain the reasoning behind their predictions.

ACTIVITY 6.

The Mysterious Ring

RESOURCES:

A large, cheap 'costume' type ring with an eye-catching stone.

PROCESS:

Tie the ring to a piece of tread and suspend it from the branch of a tree or other suitable place.   You may want to tie a label to the thread suggesting that the ring has magical powers!   Once the children have discovered it, discuss how it might have got there, who might have put nit there and what it may be capable of.   The children's responses will guide you in what direction to take the story.

ACTIVITY 7.

Whatever can it be?

RESOURCES:

Some interesting old or unusual artefacts collected from junk shops, charity shops or boot sales, e.g. a warming pan, meat mincer, old lamp etc.

PROCESS:

Conceal an item in a feely bag and let the children take turns to describe it.   If it is too big to fit in a feely bag, wrap it in an old sheet.   Once they have shared their ideas, reveal the interesting item and encourage them to speculate on what it is and what its purpose may be.

ACTIVITY 8.

The Mysterious Seeds

RESOURCES:

A packet of large seeds (<u>not beans</u>) and the story of Jack and the Beanstalk.

PROCESS:

Read or tell the story of Jack and the Beanstalk and then allow a few days to elapse.   Remove the seeds from the packet and wrap them in an interesting piece of material or paper, then put them in an envelope and post them to the children with some instructions for planting.   Encourage the children to think about who might have sent them and what they might grow into.   Plant the seeds and observe their progress!

The Old Photograph Album

RESOURCES:

An old photograph album, either genuine or 'made up'.   N.B. Old photographs are usually fairly easily acquired in junk shops / antique shops etc.)

PROCESS:

Wrap your photograph album up in some old material to give it some mystique.   Talk to the children about how you found it.   Encourage them to think about who the people might have been, whether they were related to each other and the sort of things they might have done for a living.

Include some photographs of houses, animals and places to enable you to carry the process of thinking and investigation even further.

ACTIVITY 10.

The Disappearing Cake

RESOURCES:

A simple un-iced cake bought from the supermarket.

PROCESS:

Show the cake to the children, explaining that you have bought it for a friend's birthday and would like their ideas about how you might decorate it. Once you have discussed the children's ideas place the cake on a shelf or table, and when they are out of the room remove the cake from the plate, leaving just a few crumbs behind. Then place the plate in a more prominent position for the children to discover. Once it has been found encourage the children to think about what might have happened and who or what might have eaten the cake!

ACTIVITY 11.

What is it?

RESOURCES:

A set of photographs taken from unusual angles.

PROCESS:

Take photographs of parts of your setting and the local community from unusual angles, e.g. the fire extinguisher photographed from above or below, or a door out of context.   Encourage the children to think about and identify where the photographs have been taken.   See if they can make suggestions for other things that could be photographed from unusual angles.

ACTIVITY 12.   # Who has lost these things?

RESOURCES:

A collection of things that could all belong to a famous storybook character or characters, e.g. Mrs Wishy-Washy, Mr Gumpy, Bob the Builder etc.

PROCESS:

Hide your collection of items in the outside area fro the children to discover.   Hang them from trees, drape them across hedges and conceal them in between plants.   As they are found, encourage the children to express their ideas about who the things might belong to, or which story they might fit.   Once everything has been found read the story to the children to check whether all the items fit with the story.

ACTIVITY 13.　　　　　　　# Where is it?

RESOURCES:

This activity is similar to activity 11, except that instead of photographing things from unusual angles, take photographs of prominent features in the locality. For example, the park gates, the garage forecourt, the newsagents window, etc.

PROCESS:

As with activity 11, show the photographs to the children and get them to think about and identify where the pictures have been taken. Encourage them to make their own suggestions for parts of things that would make good subjects for photographs.

ACTIVITY 14.

The Mysterious Feathers

RESOURCES:

A collection of interesting feathers that look as if they might have come from the same bird.

PROCESS:

Over time, position the feathers in prominent positions for the children to discover. Encourage them to think about whether there is anything significant about the places or times when the feathers have been found. Speculate on when the feathers may have come from, how they got into the classroom and the sort of creature they may have come from!

ACTIVITY 15.

The Spaghetti Tree

RESOURCES:

Some cooked spaghetti.

PROCESS:

Cook a packet of spaghetti and then drape it decoratively over the branches of a tree. Allow time for the children to discover it and then encourage them to think about why the spaghetti is there, how it got there and what they think should happen to it. If you tune into their ideas it will guide you in knowing where to take the story.

After some time has elapsed decorate a different tree, perhaps using noodles and see if they connect the experiences.

ACTIVITY 16.

Who owns this box?

RESOURCES:

A box of miscellaneous items donated by someone the children know and that 'give something away' about that person.

PROCESS:

Take the items out of the box one by one and see if the children can associate them with anyone they know. Encourage them to give their reasons for why they think the object belongs to a particular person. Gradually get out more items and then finally, get the children to make a decision about who the things belongs to. They can then return them to see if their deductions were correct!

ACTIVITY 17.

Who lives in a house like this?

RESOURCES:

Some photographs of a house / rooms / garden etc. donated by someone the children know.

PROCESS:

Tell the children that the object of the exercise is to figure out who lives in the house shown on the photographs. Explain that they must look for clues, e.g. do they recognise the car in the drive, the dog, the children in the garden etc. Display the photographs on the wall so that the children can look and reflect upon who might live in the house. Encourage them to give their reasons and see if they agree / disagree with each other.

ACTIVITY 18.   # The Fairy Ring

RESOURCES:

Some fairy stories, fairy pictures and a quantity of fresh mushrooms.

PROCESS:

Read some fairy stories to the children and leave some prints or pictures around for them to look at. You might even get around to talking about fairy rings! Early the next morning before the children arrive, use your cultivated mushrooms to make a fairy ring in a grassy area. When the children discover it, listen carefully to their comments and see where the line of enquiry takes you!

ACTIVITY 19.

The Button Box

RESOURCES:

A box of old buttons collected over time.

PROCESS:

Years ago, before our society became quite so 'throw away' people would cut the buttons from old clothing before getting rid of it. The buttons were usually stored in an old tin, giving countless children endless hours of pleasure. Recreate this opportunity by making your own collection of buttons. Without much encouragement the children will sort, match and pattern with them and speculate about where they might have come from. If you can get hold of them, add a few badges and medals for good measure!

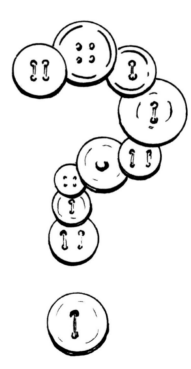

ACTIVITY 20.   # The Abandoned Briefcase

RESOURCES:
An old battered bag or briefcase containing some interesting artefacts.

PROCESS:

Conceal the briefcase or bag in a bush or behind something for the children to discover. Once they have found it, speculate on where it has come from, how it got there and who owns it. If you can borrow some things from someone and have them 'accidentally on purpose' leave them and the bag in your outside area the activity will be more exciting. The person could leave their details or phone number on something inside the bag so that the children can contact them, and see if their assumptions about who owns the bag and its contents are anything like correct!

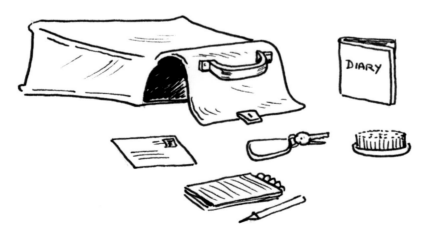

ACTIVITY 21.   # The Whispering Tree

RESOURCES:

A small portable tape recorder (that can be easily hidden).

PROCESS:

Record a repetitive message or some sound effects onto the tape recorder, conceal it in a bush and leave it playing. If the children fail to discover it, stimulate their imaginations by pointing out that <u>YOU</u> have <u>heard</u> a strange noise coming from the bushes! Encourage them to listen carefully and speculate about what might be making the noise. Eventually, once they have discovered the tape recorder they can try and figure out how the recording was made and who made it!

ACTIVITY 22.   # The Old Coins

RESOURCES:

Some old coins (foreign or otherwise).   Trowels and sieves.

PROCESS:

In a digging area of your outside area bury some old coins, leaving one or two on the surface to be discovered by the children.   Once they have found the ones on the surface pose the question of whether there might be any more underneath the ground.   Encourage them to dig carefully and systematically to see how many they can find. Get them to think about how they might have got there and who they might have belonged to.

The Stranded Cat (or Dog)

RESOURCES:

A soft toy cat or dog, and the assistance of the site manager.

PROCESS:

Position your soft toy on the roof or guttering of your setting and wait to see if the children notice it.   If they fail to do so (which is unlikely), draw their attention to it. Encourage them to think about how it got there, and more importantly, how it can be rescued. Flipchart their ideas no matter how bizarre, on the grounds that the best way to have a good idea is to have lots of ideas. Select an idea and rescue the stranded pet.

ACTIVITY 24.   # The Missing Jigsaw Pieces

RESOURCES:

A large wooden jigsaw with 6 – 10 pieces.

PROCESS:

Wrap up <u>some</u> of the jigsaw pieces in plastic bags and hide them in the outside area, hang them from branches of trees etc. for the children to discover. Once they have found some of the pieces they can make up the jigsaw as far as they can. You can then give them clues as to where the rest are hidden. These could arrive via the site manager, the cleaner, or through the post. Encourage them to guess what the picture contains as it builds up.

ACTIVITY 25.   # The hat, the glasses and the walking stick

RESOURCES:

An interesting old hat, a walking stick and a pair of spectacles (and anything else you wish to add to enhance the sense of mystery)

PROCESS:

Leave the collection of articles in the outside area. You might even add a message, e.g. 'Please Do Not Remove'. Once the children have discovered the artefacts encourage them to think about who the things might belong to. When nobody claims the items they can think about what should happen to them. On the other hand, if you know someone who is willing, they could turn up and explain to the children how and why they got left where the children had found them.

ACTIVITY 26.

The Bales of Hay (or Straw)

RESOURCES:
Some bales of hay or straw.

PROCESS:

Have some bales of hay or straw delivered to your setting. (They are great for developing physical skills in the outside area. The children can jump from one to another, and when they have exhausted the possibilities for jumping they can use the straw to make a scarecrow or a giant nest!)
However, for the purposes of this activity have the bales of hay dropped off exactly where you don't want them (within reason), e.g. right in the middle of the bike track. The object of this exercise is that of finding a way of moving the bales of hay to where you <u>do</u> want them.

Get the children to brainstorm their ideas, even if they are things that can't be accomplished without the assistance of the site manager or a team of willing helpers. The object of the exercise is that of existing the children's creative thinking.

ACTIVITY 27.　　　　　　　　**Slug Scarers and Bird Scarers**

RESOURCES:
A range of found materials etc.

PROCESS:

Next time you plant seeds or seedlings and have trouble with slugs and birds don't automatically reach for the slug pellets or the milk bottle tops. Instead, share the problem with the children and get them thinking of ways of stopping the birds pinching the seeds and the slugs nibbling the plants. See what ideas they come up with and give some of the more possible ones a try!

ACTIVITY 28.

The Everlasting Flowers

RESOURCES:

Some real and artificial flowers.

PROCESS:

Arrange some real flowers in a vase, or better still, let the children do it, as it will make them much more likely to notice them!   Surreptitiously, add some silk and plastic flowers to the display and as the real flowers fade, encourage the children to think about and comment on what is happening.

ACTIVITY 29.   **The Frozen Key**

RESOURCES:

A box that can be padlocked.   A padlock and key.   A surprise to put in the box.

PROCESS:

Before carrying out this activity with the children, place the key to the padlock in a small container of water and freeze it. To stop the key sinking to the bottom when you freeze the water, suspend it from a piece of string tied across the top of the container.

Show the children the box and explain to them that locked inside there is a surprise for them all. Go on to explain that the only trouble is that the key to the padlock is frozen inside a block of ice. Show them the block of ice with the key frozen in the middle and get them to brainstorm ideas for getting the key out and releasing the surprise.

ACTIVITY 30.

The Bunch of Keys

RESOURCES:

A bunch of keys of all shapes, sizes and ages.

PROCESS:

Tell the children that you have found / been given / collected the various keys and have tried to imagine what they belong to. Encourage them to speculate about what the keys might open. Get the children to paint pictures to go with the various keys. See whether they agree / disagree about where a certain key might have come from. Encourage them to give their reasons. Throw your own ideas into the melting pot and see how they respond to them.

ACTIVITY 31.

A box full of Coat Hangers

RESOURCES:

Would you believe … a box full of wire coat hangers, and a few assorted other types of hanger, e.g. plastic, covered, shirt hangers, trouser hangers etc.

PROCESS:

Tell the children that you have been given the box of coat hangers and have been wondering what sort of things they could be used for. Get the children to brainstorm their ideas and where possible try some of them out, e.g. they might be used to make mobiles or giant bubble blowers. Try a similar thing with a box of old plant pots or assorted lids.

ACTIVITY 32.

The Disappearing Ink

RESOURCES:

A bottle of disappearing ink bought from a joke shop. A clean white cloth.

PROCESS:

This activity really does have the children gasping in amazement! Sprinkle some disappearing ink over a clean cloth and tell the children that you don't know who has done it but that you are very annoyed about it. Ask for their ideas about how it could have happened and by the time you have finished, the ink will have disappeared. Generate ideas for how this might have happened!

ACTIVITY 33.

The Strange Lunch Box

RESOURCES:

A lunch box packed with an assortment of unusual things, e.g. jelly beans and cheese on sticks, blue tuna sandwiches (use food colouring to dye the tuna blue), iced eggs, jelly with peas set into it, etc…. (let your imagination run wild!)

PROCESS:

Explain to the children that there is a lunch box that does not seem to belong to anyone. Ask them if they have any ideas about who might have lost it. Open up the lunch box and explore the contents. Make a list of the things found inside and speculate about who might eat such a lunch.

ACTIVITY 34.

The Golden Leaves

RESOURCES:

An interesting looking plant and a can or small tin of gold paint.

PROCESS:

Show your plant to the children. Talk about who gave it to you and say how pleased you are with your new acquisition. Share ideas about where it could be placed in order to show it off to its best advantage. A day or two later carefully spray or paint one or two of the leaves gold and see how long it takes the children to notice. If they fail to notice, gentle draw their attention to the golden leaves and encourage them to offer their ideas about why the leaves have become gold. (They do say Leprechauns leave gold dust behind them!). Gradually, over time, paint more of the leaves golden. You might even add other colours. Allow the mystery to grow and see where the story takes you!

ACTIVITY 35.

Message in a Bottle

RESOURCES:

An old bottle with a cork or stopper and a suitable message or map to place inside it.

PROCESS:

Explain to the children that, you found the bottle floating in a river / canal etc when you were out walking at the weekend. Encourage them to share their ideas about who put the message in the bottle and how it can be got out. Once you have extracted the message or map, speculate on what action should be taken (this will largely be governed by the nature of the message!)

ACTIVITY 36. # The Magnificent Balloon

RESOURCES:
An incredibly large balloon.

If you are not sure how to obtain one, a good source is:
JABADAO, Branch House, 18 Branch Road, Leeds, LS12 3AQ. Telephone: 0113 231 0650.
(It is worthwhile obtaining one of their catalogues anyway as they sell super resources for movement activities!)
Jabadao sell balloons up to 36" which are great for this activity.

PROCESS:
Place the balloon in a secluded corner of the outside area or conceal it in a bush or tree.   Explain to the children that before they arrived at school you found the most amazing thing. Take them outside to see the balloon and encourage them to share their ideas about how it got there, who it belongs to and what they think should happen to it.

ACTIVITY 37.

The Birthday Present

RESOURCES:

A gift wrapped item that would be of interest to the children, e.g. sweets, a toy, a computer game etc.   The handwritten label has been badly smudged.

PROCESS:

Explain the children that you found the present on the pavement when you were walking to the shops. Draw their attention to the label and ask them to offer their ideas about how it became so smudged. Encourage them to speculate about how the present got onto the pavement, who it might belong to and who was supposed to receive it. Share thoughts about whether it should be opened or not, (the children invariably think that it should!). Talk through some alternatives about what should happen to it.

ACTIVITY 38.   **The Mysterious Picnickers**

RESOURCES:
A picnic basket and a picnic rug, crockery, cutlery, sandwiches, lemonade etc.

PROCESS:
In a secluded place outside, spread out the picnic rug and lay out the crockery, cutlery and food to look as if a group of people are having a picnic.   To make it look really authentic make sure that some of the sandwiches and cakes are half eaten. You may even like to leave a few possessions around that might belong to the picnickers.
Find an excuse for taking the children near to the picnic site or simple allow them to discover it for themselves. Once they have found the site, encourage them to offer ideas about who might have been picnicking there and why they have abandoned their picnic.

ACTIVITY 39.   # Component Parts

RESOURCES:

A collection of 'bits and pieces' gathered from familiar and not so familiar objects, e.g. half an electric plug, some nuts and bolts, the mechanism from a clock, parts of - an old radio, record player, vacuum cleaner, typewriter etc.

PROCESS:

Lay the items out on a table for the children to explore. Encourage them to observe the items carefully and support them to make connections by using open-ended questions. See how many of the items they can successfully trace back to their original source.

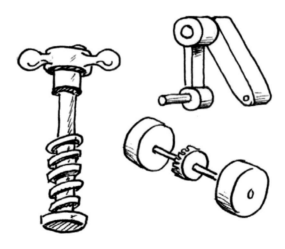

ACTIVITY 40.

The Box of Gloves

RESOURCES:

A box of assorted gloves, e.g. knitted gloves, leather gloves, mittens, fingerless gloves, lace gloves, gardening gloves, gauntlets, rubber gloves etc.

PROCESS:

Allow the children plenty of time to explore, talk about, describe and try on the gloves. Listen carefully to the comments they make as they do this and then encourage them to offer their ideas about what sort of people the gloves might belong to. You might even add some pictures of different people and see how the children match the gloves to the people. Encourage them to see that there is not necessarily any definitive right answer.

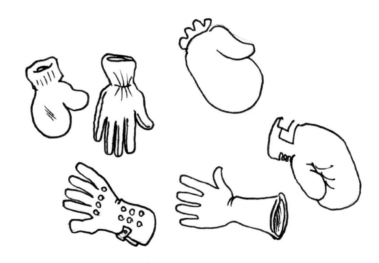

We hope you have found this publication useful. Other books in our 'Helping Young Children' series are:

Helping Young Children with STEADY BEAT	978-1-903670-26-2
Helping Young Children with PHONOLOGICAL AWARENESS	978-1-903670-73-6
Helping Young Children with NUMERACY	978-1-903670-20-0
Helping Young Children with PHONICS	978-1-903670-13-2
Helping Young Children LEARN TO READ	978-1-903670-32-3
Helping Young Children to SPEAK WITH CONFIDENCE	978-1-903670-33-0
Helping Young Children to LISTEN	978-1-903670-04-0
Helping Young Children to CONCENTRATE	978-1-903670-29-3
Helping Young Children to COME TO THEIR SENSES	978-1-903670-57-6
Helping Young Children to IMAGINE	978-1-903670-12-5
Helping Young Children to THINK CREATIVELY	978-1-903670-14-9
Helping Young Children to LEARN THROUGH MOVEMENT	978-1-903670-34-7
Helping Young Children with PSE through story	978-1-903670-45-3
Helping Young Children to ASK QUESTIONS	978-1-903670-36-1

For further information about these and our other publications, visit our website:

www.LawrenceEducational.com